BELIEFS AND CULTURES

Sikh

Catherine Chambers

W

FRANKLIN WATTS
LONDON • SYDNEY

This edition 2003

Franklin Watts
96 Leonard Street
London
EC2A 4XD

Franklin Watts Australia
45–51 Huntley Street
Alexandria
NSW 2015

Series Editor: Sarah Ridley
Designer: Liz Black
Copy Editor: Nicola Barber
Illustrator: page 27 Piers Harper; page 7 Aziz Khan
Photographer (activities): Peter Millard

Photographs: Format 6, 20, 21b, 28, 29; Hutchison
Library 15b, 17b, 18t, 21t; Ann and Bury Peerless
cover (left), 4, 13; Frank Spooner Pictures 7, 18b,
30b; Trip cover (right), 5, 8, 9, 10, 11, 14, 15t, 16,
17t, 22, 24, 25, 26, 30t.

Acknowledgements: with special thanks to Kulvant
Kaur Benning and her Panjabi class at Edgewick
Community Primary School, Coventry, England.

A CIP catalogue record for this book is available
from the British Library.
Dewey Decimal Classification Number 294.6

ISBN: 0 7496 5231 4

Printed in Dubai, UAE

CONTENTS

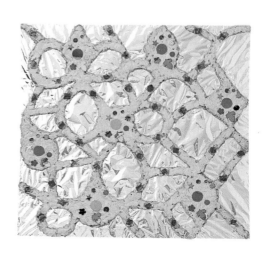

THE FIRST SIKHS

The Sikh religion is five hundred years old. It started with the teachings of Guru Nanak, the first Sikh Guru, who was born in 1469. Guru means 'religious' or 'wise teacher'. Guru Nanak was born in a small village on the flat, green plain known as the Panjab. Today, this region extends across north-west India and into Pakistan, which was created in 1947.

At the time of Guru Nanak's birth, most people in the Panjab followed one of two religions, Hinduism or Islam. Hinduism developed over 3,000 years ago in northern India.

Two Sikhs in traditional dress chat outside a *gurdwara*, or Sikh temple, in Agra, a town outside the Panjab, India.

Islam, which is practised by Muslims, began about 1,400 years ago in Arabia. It was first brought to India in 711, and by the 12th century a huge Muslim Empire ruled over the Panjab. Hindus and Muslims did not always get on well with each other. So Guru Nanak entered a world of conflict.

THE FIRST GURU

Guru Nanak was born into a Hindu family. He was a thoughtful person, deeply troubled by the divisions between people, and especially between Hindus and Muslims. Guru Nanak received messages from God, telling him to go out and teach people how to follow a simple faith.

Guru Nanak travelled far, preaching his message. Guru Nanak hoped that if people concentrated on living as God wanted them to, the differences between them would melt away. Those who followed Guru Nanak's teachings were called *Sikhs*. In the Panjabi language, 'Sikh' means 'learner'.

NEW WAYS OF THINKING

Over many years, Guru Nanak patiently told people how they could live more as God wished. He taught that people who were really trying to lead good lives should pray and meditate on God's name in a simple, humble way. They should work hard and with honesty, care for their families and serve the community. They should not gather great wealth around them.

Lots of pictures of Guru Nanak can be seen in Sikh communities around the world.

SINGING GOD'S WORD

Guru Nanak made God's teachings into poems. Mardana, one of the Guru's Muslim friends, composed and played music for them. So the poems became hymns, which were remembered and passed on.

This fresco, or wall painting, shows the young Guru Nanak left in charge of some cattle.

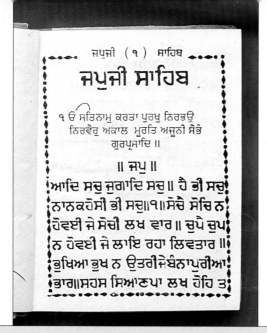

Most Sikhs will recognise this straight away! It is the *Mul Mantra*, written in *Gurmukhi* script (top three lines only).

SPOTLIGHT

Mul Mantra
This is the first and most well-known verse written by Guru Nanak. It shows how Sikhs see God, who is neither man nor woman.

There is only one God
Whose name is Truth
The Creator
Without fear
Without hate
A timeless being, not born
Self existent
Revealed only by the Guru's grace

Before he died, the Guru chose his most trusted friend, Bhai Lehna, to become the next Guru. B*hai* means 'brother' among Sikhs, and is a term showing great respect. Guru Nanak gave Lehna a new name, *Angad*, which means 'my limb'. Angad was Guru Nanak's right-hand man. The Guru also felt that Angad was a part of him, so the name suited him well. Soon after Angad had been chosen Guru Nanak died. Guru Angad was now the new teacher.

THE GURU'S TRAVELS

Guru Nanak travelled around the Panjab, teaching his message. Sometimes a small group of people gathered around him. At other times, huge crowds swarmed at his feet. Guru Nanak also made four great journeys. He travelled north into the mountains of India, and south, as far as Sri Lanka. He went westwards to Makkah and eastwards to Assam.

THE SIKH WORLD

Since then, Sikhs have also travelled taking the teachings of the Gurus with them. The first group to leave India were soldiers. They joined the British Army after Britain took over the Panjab in 1849. When the army went abroad, some Sikh soldiers decided to stay there.

INTERVIEW

We have tons of family in other countries, especially in America. I don't think their lives are much different from ours here. There aren't as many gurdwaras in America. I'd love to go there, though. Most of my cousins come from California and some live in New York.

Navpreet, aged 9, Coventry, England.

A Sikh family shows a happy mixture of traditional and Western culture in New York City, U.S.A.

For hundreds of thousands of Sikhs, the Panjab is now a foreign place. Sikh temples, called gurdwaras, have been built at the heart of Sikh communities in many countries. Some Sikhs keep traditional ways while others have more Western lifestyles. Some speak fluent Panjabi, while others speak very little. But all are Sikhs and can trace their beliefs and culture back to the Panjab and the teachings of the first Guru.

Most Sikhs who have settled outside India, live in towns and cities. Many are now moving to the cities of Europe and the Middle East.

☐ North-west border of the original Panjab area
■ Heavy Sikh populations in cities and countryside
■ Large Sikh communities, mainly in cities
■ Small Sikh communities, mainly in cities

ONLY TEN GURUS

Guru Nanak is surrounded by the other nine Gurus. You can see the youngest Guru, Guru Har Krishan, who died of smallpox in Delhi, India.

SPOTLIGHT		
THE TEN GURUS	BIRTH	DEATH
Guru Nanak	1469	1539
Guru Angad	1504	1552
Guru Amar Das	1479	1574
Guru Ram Das	1534	1581
Guru Arjan	1563	1606
Guru Hargovind	1595	1644
Guru Har Rai	1630	1661
Guru Har Krishan	1656	1664
Guru Tegh Bahadur	1621	1675
Guru Govind Singh	1666	1708

Just before Guru Nanak died, he chose Guru Angad to take his place. Eight other Gurus followed, each Guru naming his successor. The Gurus were chosen for their belief in God, their humble ways and their search for the truth. Each Guru is remembered today for giving Sikhism something special.

GURU ANGAD'S ALPHABET

Sikhs follow the teachings in the hymns composed by some of the Gurus. Today, the verses can be read, but when Guru Nanak was alive they were passed from one Sikh community to another by word of mouth.

Guru Angad, the second Guru, looked after Guru Nanak's hymns. It was not easy to remember them all, so he started to write them down. This was difficult, as there were several ways of writing the script. It is thought that Guru Angad developed the final version of the Gurmukhi alphabet, in which the hymns are still read (see page 6).

EATING TOGETHER

Sharing a meal is an important Sikh tradition. In every gurdwara, there is a dining room where people can eat together. Here everyone, Sikh or non-Sikh, is welcome. Like Guru Nanak, Guru Amar Das, the third Guru, felt that eating together was a symbol of harmony and equality. But, unlike Guru Nanak, he did not only invite people to sit and eat with him. He set up an open dining room, called a langar, where everyone was welcome. Anyone who wanted to see the Guru had first to go to the langar room and eat happily with whoever was there. The meal itself was also called langar.

Langar is sometimes eaten in a dining room with table and chairs. At the Harimandir, the huge temple in Amritsar, India, it is eaten outside.

THE GURUS BUILD A CITY FOR SIKHS

Amritsar is a city in the Indian Panjab with a magnificent temple at its heart. It was built as a place where the Gurus hymns could be stored safely. The city also became a centre of learning and culture for the Sikh community. It is visited every year by thousands of Sikhs from all over the world.

Guru Amar Das, the third Guru, started the long job of creating the city by enlarging a sacred pool, 'a pool of nectar', which is the meaning of the name 'Amritsar'. It is said that the land used by the Guru had been given to his daughter by the Muslim ruler, Emperor Akbar. The emperor had great respect for Guru Amar Das.

The pool around the temple is really a huge tank. When it is cleaned out, thousands of people come to help.

Children enjoy taking a dip in the pool in the early morning.

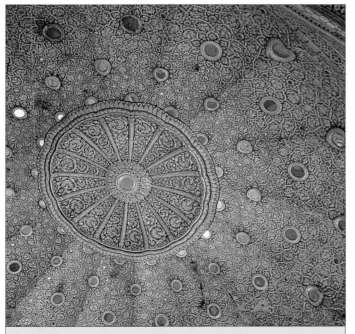

The dome of the Harimandir is lined with shining mirrors, set in gold, a style used to decorate special buildings at that time.

The Guru chose his son-in-law as the fourth Guru. It was he, Guru Ram Das, who built the city of Amritsar next to the sacred pool. Guru Ram Das's son and successor, Guru Arjan, lined the pool with bricks and built a temple in it. The temple was called Harimandir - the temple of God. It has since been rebuilt several times but now looks more or less as it did nearly 400 years ago. Today, it is also known as the Golden Temple. This is because the upper storeys were covered with copper panels gilded with gold in the 19th century.

Decorations in the Harimandir

> ## YOU WILL NEED:
>
> - thick card
> - kitchen foil
> - sequins and shiny shapes
> - bright poster paints and brushes
> - PVA glue
> - coloured cellophane sweet wrappers
> - scissors
> - newspaper and wallpaper paste or flour (for papier mâché)

WHAT TO DO:

1 Make some papier mâché by tearing up the newspaper into small pieces and soaking them in water and flour, or wallpaper paste, overnight.

2 Stick a sheet of kitchen foil smoothly over your piece of card. Squeeze the water out of the papier mâché and mould it into shapes on the card, leaving holes for the 'mirrors'. Let it dry overnight.

3 Paint the dry papier mâché a bright colour and stick on sequins and bits of coloured sweet wrappers and shiny shapes.

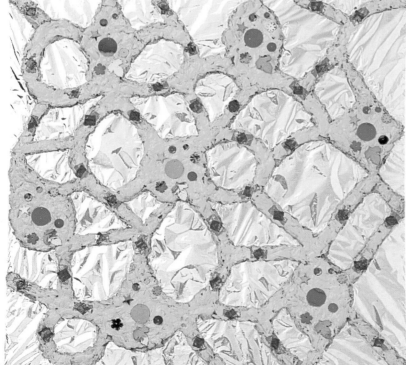

Nihang soldiers, like this one, first began as a fierce fighting force over 200 years ago.

GURU ARJAN'S IMPORTANT TASK

Guru Arjan built the Harimandir as a safe place to keep the Gurus' hymns, where no one could alter them. The Guru realised that it was best to collect the hymns together and bind them into a book. Copies could then be made for Sikhs who lived far away. So the Guru asked one of his companions, Bhai Gurdas, to gather all the Gurus' verses. They were to include the *bhagat bhani*, the hymns written by some Hindus and Muslims, whose teachings about God and life were similar to the Gurus'. The great book was compiled in 1604. Guru Arjan called it *Adi Granth*, the 'first book', meaning 'the most important'. It was placed in the Harimandir, in the hands of the first *granthi* - a person who looks after the book. Bhai Budha, an old and trusted friend of the Gurus, was given this honoured task. Today, granthis, who can be men or women, still care for the book in their gurdwaras.

13

A NEED FOR STRENGTH...

Sikhs often felt that their way of life was threatened. Sometimes they had to defend themselves against the rulers of the Panjab. A crisis came when Guru Tegh Bahadur, the ninth Guru, was killed by the Muslim emperor of India, Aurangzeb. The Guru's son, Guru Govind Singh, finally felt forced to create a Sikh army. But the army was only supposed to fight if the Sikh community was attacked.

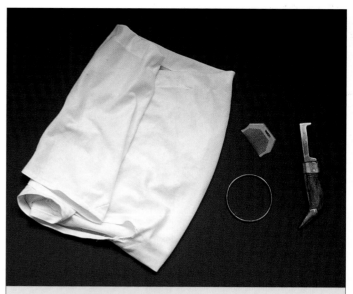

These four symbols, together with uncut hair, make up the Five 'Ks'.

... AND A NEED FOR DISCIPLINE

Each Sikh community has a group of people who promise to live by very strict rules. These men and women are identified by five special things in their appearance. The group is known as the *Khalsa*, which means 'pure'.

Guru Govind Singh chose the very first Khalsa in the town of Anandpur. The members were known as the *Panj Piare*, which means the 'five loved ones'. Guru Govind Singh knew that Sikhs needed to be as spiritually strong as their enemies if the Sikh faith and culture were going to survive.

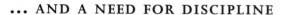

SPOTLIGHT

THE FIVE 'KS'
These are the five special things that members of the Khalsa should wear.

- *Kesh* uncut hair - a symbol of God's gifts
- *Kangha* hair-comb - to show tidiness and discipline
- *Kirpan* sword - a symbol of justice and spiritual power
- *Kachh* short trousers - to show readiness for action
- *Kara* steel wristlet - a symbol of unity and faith

The Guru gave the name *Singh* to the men in the Khalsa - this means 'lion'. He called the women *Kaur*, or 'princess'. These second names are still used by Sikhs today.

This engraving shows the very first Khalsa members drinking amrit, offered by the Guru.

The ceremony for new Khalsa members is the same today as it was for the first group. It includes drinking amrit, the 'water of life' or 'holy nectar'. This is made of sugar dissolved in water and stirred in a bowl with a short sword. It is a symbol of unity and equality.

THE LAST TASK

Guru Govind Singh knew that he was to be the last human Guru. It was now time to give over all power to God's teachings - the hymns of the Gurus. In 1706, Guru Govind Singh asked a Sikh scholar, Bhai Mani Singh, to add the hymns of Guru Tegh Bahadur to the Adi Granth. The Guru then gave the holy book a new name - the Guru Granth Sahib which means 'the volume which is the (Granth) most honoured teacher'. It is the guide and truth for all Sikhs, wherever they may be.

This is quite a new copy of the Guru Granth Sahib. The very first copy rests in a town called Kartarpur.

The Guru Granth Sahib is so precious it is wrapped in beautiful cloths and placed on a special throne in many gurdwaras.

A BOOK FOR EVERYONE

The Guru Granth Sahib is the last Guru, and the most important of all for Sikhs, because it is the Word of God. Every day, Sikhs all over the world read their holy book or recite parts of it that they know by heart. It guides and helps them in all aspects of their lives.

When the Guru Granth Sahib was first put together, only a few copies were made - all by hand. The Sikh community did not need many copies because most Sikhs lived near to one another in the Panjab. But as Sikhs began to move away, Sikh leaders realised that people might forget the teachings of the Guru Granth Sahib and be persuaded to join other religions. So, during the 19th century hundreds of copies of the Guru Granth Sahib were printed.

Schools and Khalsa colleges were set up so that the Gurmukhi script (see page 8) and Sikh teachings could be studied. As a result, Sikh culture became stronger in India and people who moved to other countries had ways of teaching Sikh traditions to their children.

All the printed Gurmukhi copies of the Guru Granth Sahib that are used for worship have 1,430 pages. The hymns are laid out in exactly the same order. This means that Sikhs throughout the world can read and learn them in the same way. There are also translations of the Guru Granth Sahib in English, French and other languages.

Students chat on their way to the Khalsa college in Amritsar, India.

A copy of the Guru Granth Sahib is being carried from a gurdwara in England to a private house for a special ceremony.

INTERVIEW

I learn the Panjabi language and the writing because I want to find out about my religion – and because my parents want me to learn.
Navpreet, aged 9, Coventry, England.

LOOKING AFTER THE BOOK

It is very important to look after the Guru Granth Sahib properly and treat it with respect. Every day in the gurdwara, the holy book is taken from its night-time resting place and put where all can see it in the main part of the temple, the Diwan hall.

The Guru Granth Sahib is wrapped in cloths called *rumalas*. Before it is read, the book is unwrapped and rested on a throne that is covered with a thick mattress and three cushions. Above the throne hangs a decorated canopy. A whisk, or *chauri*, is waved over the scriptures while they are being read.

Some people keep a copy of the Guru Granth Sahib at home. But it needs to be kept in a room of its own to give it proper respect, which not all Sikhs can afford. So many families have a small book of readings to think about through the day. The book, called a *gutka*, is wrapped in a cloth and kept on a clean, high shelf.

A copy of the gutka, resting on a clean yellow cloth as it is being read.

Waving a chauri is a sign of great respect in Indian culture.

MAKING A CHAURI

YOU WILL NEED

- *white or cream-coloured wool*
- *a stick or long pencil*
- *plasticine*   *•scissors*   *• kitchen foil*

WHAT TO DO:

1 Paint the stick or pencil with glue and cover with kitchen foil.

2 Mould the plasticine into bell shapes on the covered stick and cover with more foil.

3 Cut the wool into lengths of about 40cm.

4 Tie the strands neatly to the end of the stick with another piece of wool.

PREPARING FOR THE GURDWARA

It is important for Sikhs to treat the gurdwara with honour, so before going there, everyone takes a bath. At the entrance to the Diwan hall people remove their shoes and cover their heads. As people enter the main hall, they kneel in front of the Guru Granth Sahib and bow so that their foreheads touch the floor. After this, offerings are placed near the throne. These are often items of food which are later prepared as the langar (meal). Many people give money for charity.

When the offerings have been made, everyone sits cross-legged in front of the throne. Men and women sit in separate groups. There are no special places set aside for anyone, and there are no special priests, for everyone is meant to be treated as equal.

When Sikhs settle outside the Panjab, they often use existing buildings for their gurdwaras, as well as building new ones.

A DAY IN THE GURDWARA

The day begins very early in most gurdwaras. As early as four or five o'clock, a small group of Sikhs may carry the Guru Granth Sahib to its throne in the Diwan hall. The cloths around the holy book will be changed for clean ones. Even at this hour of the morning, there may be a small gathering of people. They will sing hymns while this ceremony, called *Parkash Karna*, takes place.

Next, the *Ardas* is spoken. This is a special prayer for guidance from

God, praising God's name. The Ardas is used on all important occasions. The Guru Granth Sahib is then opened at any page and the verse in the top left-hand corner is read aloud. This becomes the spiritual message for the day. It is called a *vak*.

The gathering then breaks up and people go about their daily work. Throughout the day, Sikhs come into the gurdwara. They receive guidance from the vak, which is written out on a notice board. Some people arrange meetings in one of the small rooms in the gurdwara. Others eat in the langar room, joining whoever is sitting there. The gurdwara is a place for meeting up with people as well as for worship.

Everyone sits down to listen and sing in the gurdwara. Children are not expected to be quiet!

The langar can be a very busy place. Huge cooking pots are needed to hold enough food for everyone there.

In the evening, some Sikhs gather in the gurdwara for the last ceremony of the day. A song of praise, *Kirtan Sohila*, is read out and a prayer is spoken. The Guru Granth Sahib is closed and wrapped in a white cloth. One Sikh covers his or her head with a rumala and carries the holy book away on top of it. A procession

In Delhi, India, children are playing music inside the gurdwara, which can be used for various events.

Karah parsad is being given out at the Harimandir in Amritsar, India. The person receiving it always makes a bow.

follows, led by someone slowly waving a chauri. Everyone chants a special hymn as the scriptures are taken to their resting place for the night.

For the family gathering at the gurdwara, Sikh communities use the official rest day of the country in which they live. So in Canada, the United States and Britain, for example, the family day at the gurdwara is on Sunday. On this day, people come to the gurdwara when they can and leave when they need to. But most try to stay until the Ardas is sung and the Guru Granth Sahib is opened to give the vak. Then everyone receives a small amount of sweet mixture that has been stirred in a bowl by a short sword (kirpan) during the Ardas. They eat this offering, called karah parsad, just as they are leaving the Diwan hall to go to the langar room.

MAKING KARAH PARSAD

YOU WILL NEED

- 200 gms of semolina
- 200 gms of sugar
- 200 gms of ghee or unsalted butter
- saucepan
- wooden spoon
- half a cup of water

♣ Ask for help from an adult with this activity.

WHAT TO DO:

1 Wash your hands. Then melt the ghee or butter in a pan over a low heat.

2 Add the semolina and cook it for 6 or 7 minutes until it is golden brown. Keep stirring so that it does not stick to the pan.

3 Mix the sugar in well and add the water, cooking slowly until the mixture thickens. Watch out for steam.

4 Dish it up in a shiny bowl and share with your friends.

This is a turban shop, full of bright lengths of cloth, in Amritsar, India.

BUSY LIVES

Sikhism is a way of life, not just a way of worship. Sikh communities have to survive and work in the modern world just like every other. But many Sikhs try to include prayer and meditation in their everyday lives, so that they will remember God's Name. For some, this means spending some part of the day at the gurdwara. For others, it could mean meditating at home before breakfast and on the way to work or school.

DRESSING DIFFERENTLY

It is often difficult to tell if someone belongs to the Sikh community or not. Many Sikhs have short, uncovered hair and wear Western dress, particularly in the United States, Canada and Britain. But a lot of people will show that they are Sikhs by not cutting any body hair, as Guru Govind Singh requested. Young boys have a small cloth to cover the hair until they learn to tie a turban.

Steel bracelets are sold on a souvenir stall owned by Sikhs, near the Harimandir in Amritsar, India.

Some women and young girls dress in long tunics and trousers, known as *salwar kamiz*. Their hair is uncut but usually tied back. Many Sikhs, both men and women, wear a kara, or steel bracelet. It reminds them of their faith throughout the day.

THE WORLD OF WORK

The Gurus stressed the importance of work to their followers. They especially encouraged people to set up their own businesses. In India, some traditional occupations for Sikhs were farming, building and working as mechanics. But nowadays, Sikhs all over the world take up every kind of job or profession.

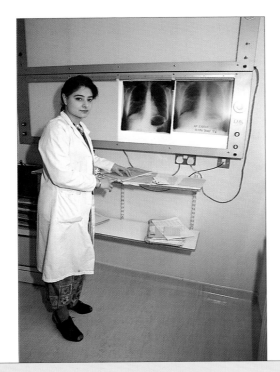

In England, a Sikh doctor is examining X-rays. Sikh men and women enter all professions.

The traditional skills of carpenters are still highly valued. These Sikhs own a carpenter's shop in Amritsar, India.

This cafe has bright pictures of the Gurus around the walls. You will see them in many Sikh shops, offices and homes.

EATING AND DRINKING

Some Sikhs choose to be vegetarians. This is mainly because Sikhism began where there were large Hindu communities, and Hindus do not normally eat meat. The Gurus advised Sikhs to respect the rules of the people around them. The rules for eating are not very strict. But Guru Govind Singh gave very strong reasons why no one should drink alcohol, smoke tobacco or take drugs. The Guru said that they are harmful to our bodies and our minds.

Outside India, some children go to the gurdwara after school for lessons to learn Panjabi and the Gurmukhi script.

AFTER SCHOOL

Sikh children do not only do their homework, play games or watch television after school. Many go to the gurdwara to practise singing hymns. Some learn to play musical instruments to accompany them. Outside India, the Panjabi language has to be taught at home and in the gurdwara. Learning the Gurmukhi script is difficult, but the Guru Granth Sahib cannot be read without it.

SOMETHING TO THINK ABOUT – Children often learn about their culture through listening to stories. The Gurus told their followers many stories. Some are really messages, explaining difficult ideas and decisions. Others are about the lives of the Gurus and the wonderful deeds they performed. These help to explain Sikh history.

This is a good story to think about as people go about their busy lives. It happened on Guru Nanak's long journey to the south.

At one place where he stopped, Guru Nanak was visited by a man called Duni Chand and his wife. Duni Chand was extremely rich. But like a lot of rich people, he occasionally wanted the approval of someone holy. So he came to pay his respects to Guru Nanak. Just as he was leaving, Guru Nanak pulled a needle from his bag and gave it to Duni Chand, saying,

"Could you keep this safely for me? When I die, you can give it to me in the next world."

Duni Chand was a bit puzzled. "But how can anyone carry a needle into the next world?" he asked. "Then why have you collected all these riches if you can't take them with you?" replied the Guru.

Duni Chand and his wife realised what Guru Nanak was trying to tell them. They went home and gave away all their riches. And from then on, everything that they earned, they shared.

FAMILY FESTIVALS

Sikhs share the special joys of family life with the whole community. Birth and marriage are welcomed with lively celebrations as well as gratitude to God.

Naming the baby in the gurdwara is one of the happiest and most important celebrations of all.

A NEW MEMBER

When a baby is born into a Sikh family, the baby's father tells the happy news to friends and relatives - he gives out boxes of sweets, too! Presents of clothes and money are brought to the baby.

After two weeks, the baby is usually taken to the gurdwara on the day of the family gathering for the naming ceremony. The parents often bring new rumalas to cover the Guru Granth Sahib. After hymns of praise and thanks to God, the parents promise to bring up the new baby as a Sikh.

One person turns to the Guru Granth Sahib and sings the Ardas. The baby is laid in front of the scriptures while the granthi opens them to read the verse in the top left-hand corner. The first letter of the verse becomes the beginning letter of the baby's name. Now the parents can choose a name for their child, with much prompting from the rest of the people gathered there! The new name is followed with 'Singh' if the child is a boy or 'Kaur' if it is a girl (see page 15). When the granthi announces the name, everyone shouts the Sikh words of greeting, "Sat-Sri-Akal!" - "God is truth!"

GETTING MARRIED

The Gurus taught that family life is very important. So getting married is a very serious business. Parents often help their children to choose a partner. The couple must be able to live together happily, so they discuss what they enjoy doing, the places they like visiting and the things they believe in.

The bride's father has tied his daughter's scarf to the bridegroom's scarf, to show that she has left her own family.

In India, Sikhs have only the religious ceremony. Elsewhere, most attend ceremonies at the gurdwara, the registry office, or both. The wedding hymn by Guru Ram Das is the central part of the gurdwara ceremony. It is known as the *Lavan*. The couple walk clockwise around the Guru Granth Sahib as each of the four verses is sung.

ANNIVERSARIES

Festivals known as *gurpurbs* mark anniversaries. The births of Guru Nanak and Guru Govind Singh are honoured in this way. In the gurdwaras, activities begin two days before the gurpurb with an *Akhand Path*. This continuous reading of the Guru Granth Sahib stops very early

Five members of the Khalsa, dressed in the five 'Ks', always lead processions held at gurpurbs.

on the morning of the gurpurb. Many people gather to hear the last verses of the scriptures. They also listen to special readings and talks about the Guru who is being remembered.

Vaisakhi is also the day when Guru Govind Singh chose the members of the Khalsa. Here it is being celebrated with a fighting ritual.

SHARING FESTIVALS

Some Sikh festivals are held at the same time as Hindu ones. Sikhs and Hindus share some of the same ways of celebrating. But the Gurus gave each of these festivals a special meaning for their followers.

HAPPY NEW YEAR!

Sikhs celebrate New Year's Day, or *Vaisakhi*, on the same day as Hindus. Traditionally, it celebrates the end of the spring wheat harvest in the Panjab.

A FESTIVAL OF LIGHT

Diwali is probably the most spectacular of all celebrations for Sikhs and Hindus. It marks the end of the hot season and the start of winter, when crops can be sown. But Hindu religious stories also show that it is a time when good overcomes evil and light pushes away the darkness.

For Sikhs, Diwali marks the day when Guru Hargovind was released from prison. As the Guru made his way back to Amritsar, Sikh houses shone with candlelight, lit in celebration of his return.

On Diwali, everyone has great fun in the streets as fireworks explode into the night. Small clay lamps, or *diwas*, glow all around.

MAKING A SIKH FLAG

YOU WILL NEED

- *a stick, 70cm long, dowelling is best*
- *a triangle of orange cloth, 35cm on all sides*
- *a large square of orange cloth, 50cm by 50cm*
- *a square of blue cloth, 20cm by 20cm*
- *a square of paper, 20cm by 20cm*
- *a small piece of cooking foil and card*
- *PVA glue and brush, a pencil and a pair of scissors*

The two edged sword (khanda), quoit (chakar) and sword (kirpan). These are symbols of unity, faith and brotherhood.

WHAT TO DO:

1 On your square of paper, draw and cut out the symbols shown above right. Pin them on the blue material and cut them out.

2 Stick the fabric symbols on to the orange triangle with PVA glue.

3 Fold the side of the orange triangle round the stick. Glue it down at the back. Make a khanda symbol from card covered with foil. It should be 10cm tall. Glue to the top of the stick.

The flag is respected as one of the symbols of the Sikh faith. So, unless you are using it, cover it with the large piece of orange cloth.

GLOSSARY

Adi Granth 'the first book' - 'the most important book' for Sikhs; the first collection of the hymns of Gurus and other saints

Akhand Path a continuous reading of the Gurus' scriptures, used on special occasions

amrit 'water of life' or 'holy nectar'; sweetened water used in Khalsa initiation

Ardas a prayer for guidance

bhagat bhani hymns written by some Hindus and Muslims

chauri a whisk waved in respect over the Guru Granth Sahib

Five 'Ks' the five symbols worn by members of the Khalsa

granthi someone who takes care of the Book

gurdwara a Sikh place of worship

Gurmukhi the writing in the scriptures and modern Panjabi

gurpurb a festival to mark an anniversary of the birth or death of a guru

Guru one of the ten teachers and guides of Sikhs

Guru Granth Sahib the final collection of the Adi Granth and the bhagat bhani

gutka a small book of hymns and prayers

Harimandir the 'Temple of god' in Amritsar

karah parsad a special, blessed, sweetmeat given out in the gurdwara

Kaur 'Princess' - a name given to Sikh girls

Khalsa the 'Pure ones' - forming a group of specially dedicated Sikhs

langar the dining room in the gurdwara, or the meal eaten there

Lavan a hymn always sung at weddings

Mul Mantra the first verse written by the first Guru, Guru Nanak

Panjabi the language used by Sikhs and others from the Panjab - sometimes spelled 'Punjabi'

rumalas cloths covering the Guru Granth Sahib

Singh 'Lion' - a name given to Sikh boys

vak a daily spiritual message to help people through the day

INDEX